THE FUN-TO-LEARN
PICTURE
ENCYCLOPEDIA

The Solar System

Venus

Jupiter

Sun

Mars

Uranus

Earth

Pluto

Saturn

Neptune

Mercury

The Planets

There are nine planets that circle the Sun. Together they are called the solar system. Our Earth is one of the smaller planets.

Our solar system is made up of nine planets that travel in orbit around the Sun. They are Mercury, Venus, Earth, Mars, Jupiter, Saturn, Uranus, Neptune and Pluto, together with a ring of asteroids. These are thousands of pieces of rock between Mars and Jupiter.

The Sun is the biggest thing we can see when we look into the sky. It is a huge star that gives out heat and light. The planets produce no light of their own and, like the Earth, get their warmth and light from the Sun.

The Sun

The Sun's diameter is 100 times bigger than the Earth's. It is really just a ball of super hot gas. The temperature at the centre of the Sun is 15,000,000°C and it is 5,500°C on the surface.

The Earth is 149,637,000 km (93,000,000 miles) from the Sun. If we were any nearer, it would be too hot and all life would die out.

You must never look directly at the Sun with a telescope or binoculars as the brightness would damage your eyes.

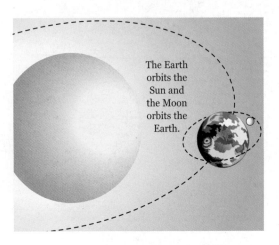

The Earth orbits the Sun and the Moon orbits the Earth.

2800°C

800°C

100°C

Mercury
58 million km (36 million miles) from the Sun, no moon, orbits the Sun every 88 days.

Venus
108 million km (67 million miles) from the Sun, no moon, orbits the Sun every 225 days.

Earth
150 million km (93 million miles) from the Sun, one moon, orbits the Sun every 365 1/4 days.

Mars
228 million km (142 million miles) from the Sun, two moons, orbits the Sun every 687 days.

Jupiter
778 million km (480 million miles) from the Sun, 16 moons, orbits the Sun every 11.86 years.

Saturn
1,427 million km (886 million miles) from the Sun, 17 moons, orbits the Sun every 29.46 years.

Uranus
2,870 million km (1,783 million miles) from the Sun, 15 moons, orbits the Sun every 84 years.

Neptune
4,500 million km (2,800 million miles) from the Sun, three moons, orbits the Sun every 165 years.

Pluto
5,970 million km (3,700 million miles) from the Sun, one moon, orbits the Sun every 248 years.

The Earth

Earth is the planet on which we all live. Scientists believe that about 5,000 million years ago, a swirling mass of boiling hot rocks and gases, revolving around the Sun, changed into a ball of liquid rock that formed the Earth.

Very slowly, over hundreds of millions of years, the Earth cooled down and a hard crust formed on the outside.

Sometimes the hot gases and liquid broke through the crust, moving and cracking the surface. This formed mountains and cut deep trenches that later formed the ocean beds.

Millions of years went by, the Earth became cooler and great clouds of vapour covered the Earth and fell as rain. This made the rivers and lakes and filled up the seas and oceans.

Scientists believe that all the continents were once joined together in one great mass called Pangaea. This broke up and formed the continents that we know today.

If your bathroom scales were big enough you would find that the Earth weighed about 6,000 million, million, million tonnes! The Earth's 'waist' measurement, round the equator, is over 40,000 km (24,856 miles).

The Moon

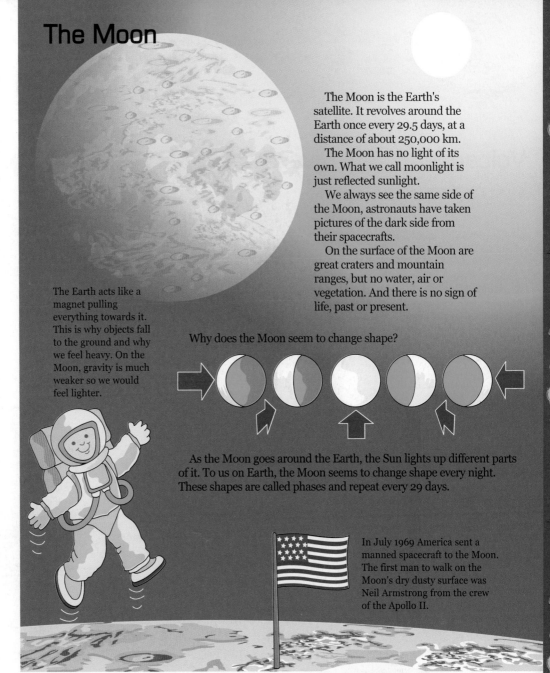

The Moon is the Earth's satellite. It revolves around the Earth once every 29.5 days, at a distance of about 250,000 km.

The Moon has no light of its own. What we call moonlight is just reflected sunlight.

We always see the same side of the Moon, astronauts have taken pictures of the dark side from their spacecrafts.

On the surface of the Moon are great craters and mountain ranges, but no water, air or vegetation. And there is no sign of life, past or present.

The Earth acts like a magnet pulling everything towards it. This is why objects fall to the ground and why we feel heavy. On the Moon, gravity is much weaker so we would feel lighter.

Why does the Moon seem to change shape?

As the Moon goes around the Earth, the Sun lights up different parts of it. To us on Earth, the Moon seems to change shape every night. These shapes are called phases and repeat every 29 days.

In July 1969 America sent a manned spacecraft to the Moon. The first man to walk on the Moon's dry dusty surface was Neil Armstrong from the crew of the Apollo II.

Did you know that three-quarters of our planet is covered by water?

The highest point on the Earth's surface is Mount Everest, 8,848m (29,030 feet) high, but the deepest part of the ocean, the Mariana Trench, is 11,033m (36,199 feet) deep.

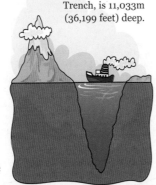

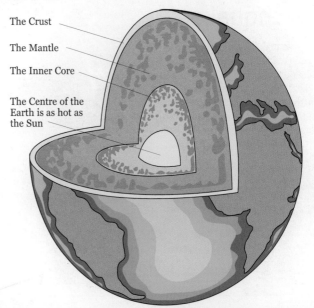

The Crust

The Mantle

The Inner Core

The Centre of the Earth is as hot as the Sun

Our earth is always slowly changing. The sea, the rain, the wind and the frost break down the rocks and wear away the surface. This happens very slowly. It is called erosion.

Volcanoes

Some changes to the planet happen suddenly! Although the Earth feels cool on the surface, it is very hot inside.

Sometimes the lava and gases find a weak spot in the Earth's crust and suddenly burst through. Ash, red-hot cinders and boiling lava spread over the land, often covering entire towns.

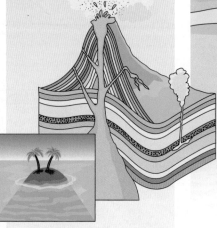

Some volcanoes erupt under the sea. After a while, when the lava cools, a new island may be formed.

Earthquakes

Earthquakes often happen in those parts of the world where volcanoes occur.

The rock deep beneath the Earth's surface moves, then splits and cracks appear along a weak point in the Earth's crust.

Rivers

Rivers begin in mountains or hills as small trickles of rainwater or melting snow. Trickles flow together to form streams and these join other streams to form a river. The river becomes slower and broader as it winds across the land and reaches the sea or lake at the river's mouth.

When a river comes to the edge of a cliff it plunges down, forming a waterfall.

A glacier is a slow-moving river of ice. It creeps down the valley taking large rocks with it. It melts as it reaches the warmer, lower lands.

The Grand Canyon

This has been cut out of the solid rock by the Colorado River over millions of years. It is up to 1.6 km (1 mile) deep

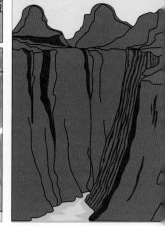

A big earthquake can cause enormous waves in the sea. These huge tidal waves can cause terrible floods, often many miles inland.

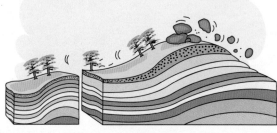

The Earth's Climate

The words 'weather' and 'climate' have quite different meanings. When someone tells you that it has been warm and sunny that day, they are talking about the weather.

If they say the Sahara Desert is always hot and the Arctic is always cold, they are talking about the climate of these places, which has been the same for a very long time.

Temperature, rainfall, winds and ocean currents all affect a region's climate. And the distance from the equator, northwards or southwards, determines whether the area is hot or cold.

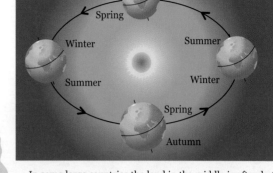

The temperature falls as you go up a mountain. There are mountains on the equator, the hottest part of the Earth, with snow on their peaks all the year round.

Australia

In some large countries the land in the middle is often hot and dry. The moist winds from the sea never reach inland, so there is very little rainfall.

Cold Zone North

Cool Zone

Warm Zone

Hot Zone

Warm Zone

Cold Zone South

North Pole

South Pole

As the Earth spins around the Sun it tilts on its axis. Near the equator the Sun is almost overhead, so it is always hot and the rays are very strong.

As they spread out towards the poles over a wider area, the Sun's rays are weaker and the land is cooler.

5

The Tropical Rainforest

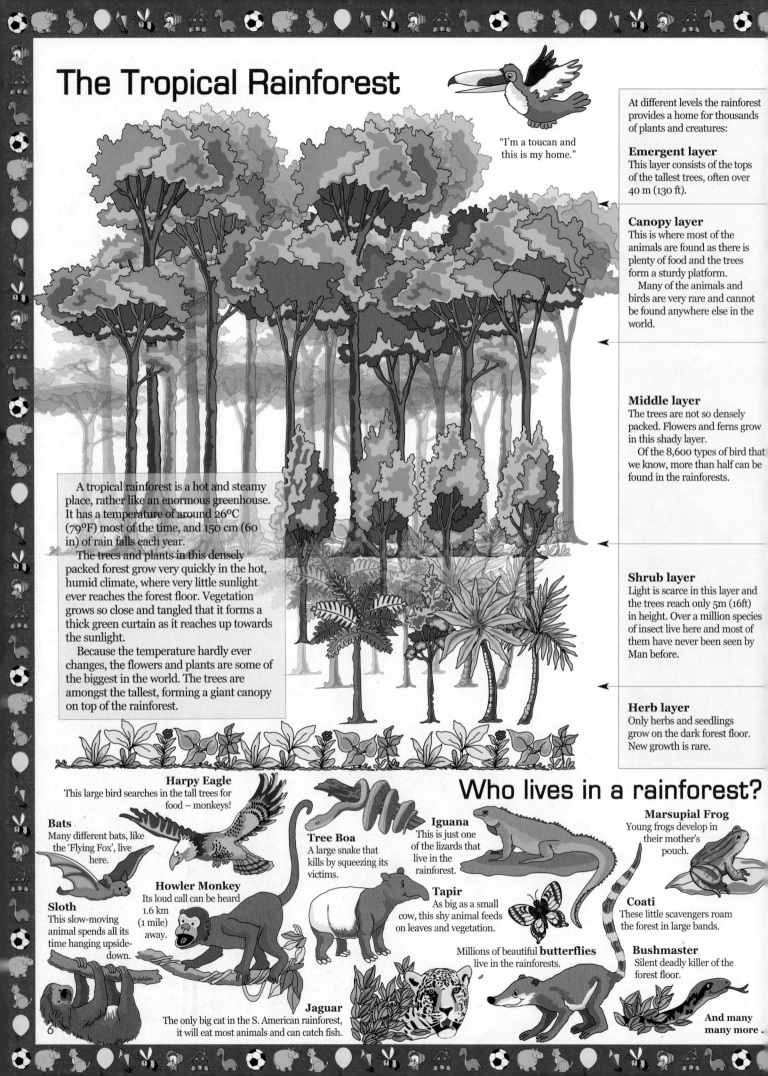

"I'm a toucan and this is my home."

At different levels the rainforest provides a home for thousands of plants and creatures:

Emergent layer
This layer consists of the tops of the tallest trees, often over 40 m (130 ft).

Canopy layer
This is where most of the animals are found as there is plenty of food and the trees form a sturdy platform.
    Many of the animals and birds are very rare and cannot be found anywhere else in the world.

Middle layer
The trees are not so densely packed. Flowers and ferns grow in this shady layer.
    Of the 8,600 types of bird that we know, more than half can be found in the rainforests.

Shrub layer
Light is scarce in this layer and the trees reach only 5m (16ft) in height. Over a million species of insect live here and most of them have never been seen by Man before.

Herb layer
Only herbs and seedlings grow on the dark forest floor. New growth is rare.

A tropical rainforest is a hot and steamy place, rather like an enormous greenhouse. It has a temperature of around 26ºC (79ºF) most of the time, and 150 cm (60 in) of rain falls each year.
    The trees and plants in this densely packed forest grow very quickly in the hot, humid climate, where very little sunlight ever reaches the forest floor. Vegetation grows so close and tangled that it forms a thick green curtain as it reaches up towards the sunlight.
    Because the temperature hardly ever changes, the flowers and plants are some of the biggest in the world. The trees are amongst the tallest, forming a giant canopy on top of the rainforest.

Who lives in a rainforest?

Harpy Eagle
This large bird searches in the tall trees for food – monkeys!

Bats
Many different bats, like the 'Flying Fox', live here.

Tree Boa
A large snake that kills by squeezing its victims.

Iguana
This is just one of the lizards that live in the rainforest.

Marsupial Frog
Young frogs develop in their mother's pouch.

Sloth
This slow-moving animal spends all its time hanging upside-down.

Howler Monkey
Its loud call can be heard 1.6 km (1 mile) away.

Tapir
As big as a small cow, this shy animal feeds on leaves and vegetation.

Coati
These little scavengers roam the forest in large bands.

Millions of beautiful **butterflies** live in the rainforests.

Bushmaster
Silent deadly killer of the forest floor.

Jaguar
The only big cat in the S. American rainforest, it will eat most animals and can catch fish.

And many many more .

6

Where do you find the rainforests?

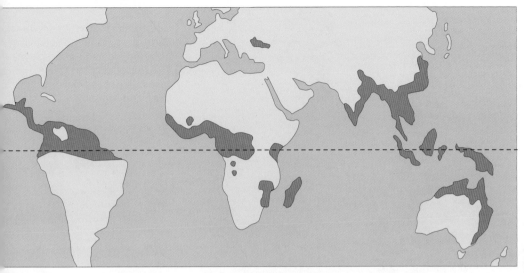

They stretch around the Equator, with at least half of them in Central and South America. There the world's biggest rainforest covers over 6.5 million sq km (2.5 million sq miles). The River Amazon flows through this forest for more than half its length, over 3,220 km (2,000 miles). Often the only way to travel through the dense forest is by river.

More rainforest can be found in West Africa, Madagascar, Sri Lanka, Burma, Malaysia, Indonesia, New Guinea and Australia.

What is happening to the rainforests?

In the last few years, great areas of forest have been destroyed as people have moved in, We have cut down the trees for timber, dug great holes in the Earth to find minerals, and burned and cleared the forest for farming.

Not only do animals and birds live in the forest, people live there as well. When the forest is destroyed, their land and homes are gone too.

Most of us will never be able to visit a rainforest, but some of the flowers and plants can be seen in the big heated glasshouses at botanical gardens.

There are over five billion people on the earth and the number is growing all the time. In fact, there are 150 babies born across the world every minute!

Polluting the land, sea and air, killing the wildlife and destroying the forests affects every one of us. It upsets the delicate balance of nature on which we all depend.

A quarter of all the drugs and medicines prescribed by doctors come from plants found in the rainforest.

Rainforests contain half of all known types of world creature.

No-one wants our planet to die, so everyone must work hard to look after all life on Earth.

Why do we need rainforests?

Trees and plants have a very important part to play in keeping the Earth's air supply pure. If we destroyed all the forests, there would be no trees left to take the carbon dioxide and give out the oxygen that we need to breathe, This would cut off the world's air supply.

Many people think of the rainforest as the Earth's lungs!

We breathe in oxygen and breathe out carbon dioxide. Plants use this carbon dioxide to make more oxygen.

7

The Weather

We have no way of controlling the weather. It changes all the time. Too much sunshine – not enough rain – storms and winds – frost and snow! These are all part of the Earth's weather and can change from hour to hour, or day to day.

What makes the weather change?

As the heat of the Sun reaches the Earth, it warms the air and makes it move around in the atmosphere. This causes the wind to blow, water vapour to rise and clouds to form to make rain and snow.

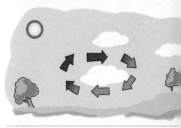

What is atmosphere?

The Earth is covered with a layer of air called the atmosphere. As you move further away from the Earth the air gets thinner.

Near the ground breathing is easy. If you climb up a high mountain there is less oxygen, so it is harder to breathe. Higher up still, in an aeroplane, the air is so thin that the cabin is pressurised (air is pumped in) so the passengers can breathe.

The atmosphere is a thick blanket of air wrapped round the Earth, protecting it from the fierce heat of the Sun by day, and keeping the warmth near the Earth at night.

Different clouds mean different weather

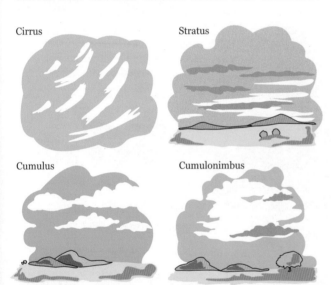

Cirrus

Stratus

Cumulus

Cumulonimbus

Cirrus
The highest clouds of all. Made of specks of ice, they have wispy, feathery shapes. Sometimes they are called 'mare's-tails'.

Stratus
Thin, low layers of grey cloud that often cover high ground. They usually bring drizzle.

Cumulus
Low, fluffy white clouds, like heaps of cotton wool that drift across the sky. They bring fine weather and sunny spells.

Cumulonimbus
Towering clouds like billowing smoke that reach high up into the sky. If the clouds are heavy and dark, a thunderstorm may be close by!

It's the same old rain again!

All life on Earth depends on light from the Sun, but it also depends on an endless supply of water.

Did you know that the same old rain falls to Earth over and over again?

When warm winds blow over oceans or seas, the water on the top evaporates. This moisture then rises to form clouds in the sky.

As the clouds are blown over mountains or hills by wind, they become cool. The moisture forms water droplets that fall back down to Earth as rain.

The rain runs into streams, then rivers and is carried back to the sea – to start all over again !

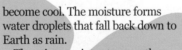

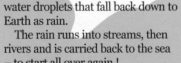

Mount Everest

Hailstones

Hailstones are raindrops that freeze as they fall through layers of very cold air.

When they fall down from the sky, hailstones are usually as big as peas. Sometimes they can be as big as tennis balls – so watch out!

Fog

Fog is cloud that is near the ground instead of up in the sky. It forms when damp air cools and hangs in the air. When the fog is thick, you can't see very well.

Snow

When water vapour in the clouds freezes it makes tiny ice crystals. These join together to form snowflakes.

If you look at a snowflake through a magnifying glass, you will see that these beautiful crystals form six-sided patterns. You will never find two the same – however hard you look!

Dew

On clear cloudless nights some of the Earth's warmth is lost in the atmosphere. The air near the ground cools and forms little drops of water that we call dew. If the temperature is below freezing the dew becomes frost.

Lightning and Thunder

Lightning is a huge electric spark passing between two clouds or travelling from a cloud to the Earth.

The loud crack of thunder we hear is the noise made by the giant spark, as the air expands round it.

Lightning and thunder happen at the same time, but you see the flash before you hear the thunder, because light travels faster than sound.

Tall trees and buildings are often struck by lightning. Never stand under a tree during a thunderstorm.

How do we measure the weather?

Weather Satellite
This orbits the earth at a height of 700 km (434 miles) and sends back pictures of clouds and weather patterns.

Windsock
This shows which way the wind is blowing.

Rain Gauge
This measures the amount of rain that has fallen.

Anemometer
This measures the wind speed.

Sunshine Recorder
This measures the hours of sunshine in a day.

Thermometer
This tells us how high or low the temperature is.

Barometer
This measures the pressure of the atmosphere.

Wind

Can you see the wind? Of course not! Wind is just air moving around. The wind can be a gentle breeze or a fierce hurricane blowing at a speed of 120 kph (75 mph). When the Earth's surface is warm, the air above it is heated and rises. Then cool air flows in to take its place. That movement of air is called wind.

The Beaufort Scale

This was devised in 1806 by Admiral Beaufort of the British Royal Navy who used numbers to describe wind strengths.

When the weatherperson says 'force 9 on the Beaufort scale', you know they mean a strong gale.

Force	Strength	Kph
0	Calm	0-1
1	Light air	1-5
2	Light Breeze	6-11
3	Gentle breeze	12-19
4	Moderate breeze	20-29

Force	Strength	Kph
5	Fresh breeze	30-39
6	Strong breeze	40-50
7	Near Gale	51-61

Force	Strength	Kph
8	Gale	62-74
9	Strong Gale	75-87
10	Storm	88-101

Force	Strength	Kph
11	Violent storm	102-117
12	Hurricane	118+

Life Begins on Earth

Millions of years ago, the Earth was a mass of hot rocks and gases. As the Earth cooled, the huge cloud of steam that covered the planet turned to water. Then it fell as rain, cooling the Earth even more, forming the rivers, seas and oceans.

Over many more millions of years, the first forms of plant life began to grow in the sea. In time, simple animals evolved too: sponges, sea-snails and, eventually, fish.

Later on, plants started to grow by the edge of the water. Some sea creatures grew legs to walk on land and lungs to breathe in the air. Reptiles were the first creatures to breed on land, and some of the insects developed wings and could fly.

In the Earth's warm steamy atmosphere, plants, insects and reptiles grew bigger and bigger – especially dinosaurs.

How do we know this happened?

The remains of plants, shells and bones of prehistoric creatures have been found millions of years later, preserved in stone. They are called fossils.

Fossils are found in layers of rock all over the world. The oldest ones are in the bottom layers, with the newer ones at the top.

Some fossils are quite small, such as a leaf preserved in rock. Others may be the whole skeleton of a dinosaur – the largest creature that ever walked on Earth!

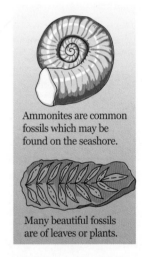

Ammonites are common fossils which may be found on the seashore.

Many beautiful fossils are of leaves or plants.

Putting together bits of a creature no-one has ever seen before is like doing a jigsaw puzzle without the picture. Sometimes scientists must get it wrong!

The first out of the water

The first creatures to come out of the water were the lobe-finned fish that were developing lungs.

The first amphibian was the Ichthyostega that had strong legs for walking on land. It may have begun to leave the water searching for food in dry times.

Ichthyostega

Finding a fossilised dinosaur skeleton is exciting work, especially extracting all the pieces from the rock in which they have lain for millions of years.

The Dinosaurs

Although dinosaurs are now extinct, they lived all over the world for 160 million years. Human beings have lived on the Earth for just 35,000 years.

Some dinosaurs were huge creatures, the largest animals that ever walked the Earth, Others were small not much bigger than a chicken!

Brontosaurus
Brontosourus means 'thunder lizard' and this huge animal was 21m (69ft) long and lived 200 million years ago. It fed on vegetation, probably reaching in trees with its enormous neck.

Allosaurus
At 13m (43ft) long and weighing over two tonnes, this fierce meat-eater was definitely one to avoid 200 million years ago.

Dryosaurus
This plant eater was 3m (10ft) long and would need all of its speed to avoid the Allosaurus.

Dimetrodon
This strange creature lived 285 million years ago.
The sail on its back probably helped to control body temperature. At 3.5m (11ft) in length, it was a predator feeding on smaller animals.

Delonosuchus
Seventy-five million years ago this huge crocodile grew to a length of 16m (52ft).

Agathaumus
Remains of this well-protected animal from 65 million years ago have been found in Wyoming in America.

Plesiosaurus
Skeletons of this 5m (16ft) long creature was found on the coast of England over 200 years ago. Many people believe that this is the famous Loch Ness monster from Scotland, although it lived over 200 million years ago.

Euparkeria
This chicken-sized dinosaur lived 245 million years ago. Although very small, it was a fast moving meat-eater.

Ichthyosaurus
Dolphin-like, but much bigger at 10m (33ft), this fish-eater roamed the seas 225 million years ago.

Pteranodon

Living about 100 million years ago, this creature had a huge wing span of 7.5m (25ft). It was not a true flier, but a glider. The flat horn on the back of its head acted like a rudder.

Archaeopteryx

This feathered dinosaur was probably the ancestor of the birds. About the size of a crow, this creature lived in the Jurassic period, 195-135 million years ago.

Triceratops

This was the largest of the horned dinosaurs.

Weighing around 6 tonnes, and 9m (30ft) in length, it was a vegetarian well able to defend itself against the big predators.

Stegosaurus

The big plates on the back of this 1.5 tonne animal were probably used to control body temperature rather than for defence. A harmless plant-eater, it was about 8m (26ft) in length.

Deinonychus

The name means 'terrible claw'. Although only as tall as a man, this fast moving hunter had a terrible weapon – a 12cm (4 1/2 in) claw on the first toe of each foot that it would use to disembowel its prey.

Why did the dinosaurs die out?

Dinosaurs roamed the Earth for about 160 million years. Then about 65 million years ago they vanished. No-one really knows why.

Some scientists think that a huge meteor hit the Earth and started volcanic eruptions – the dust and ash would have blotted out the Sun for years. Or perhaps the Earth's climate grew much colder and the cold-blooded dinosaurs could not stand the cold as well as the warm-blooded mammals that had begun to live on Earth.

"I don't think I would like to have met this one!"

Tyrannosaurus Rex

The king of the dinosaurs! This giant beast lived about 100 million years ago. It stood 5m (16ft) tall and 14m (45ft) long. Rather than killing its own prey it survived by frightening smaller dinosaurs from their kill.

Plants

Flowers are the parts of a plant that make seeds to grow new plants.

A plant is a living thing made up of cells. All plants must have sunlight, air, water and food to live and grow. We get our energy from eating food. A plant can make food for itself.

New plants grow from the seeds produced by the old plant. When you plant a seed in the soil, it will begin to grow, or 'germinate' so long as it has water, warmth and air.

The green leaves trap energy from the sun and, together with carbon dioxide from the air and water from the soil, make sugar, which is the plant's food.

carbon dioxide

Plants take in carbon dioxide and give out oxygen.

oxygen

Sap rises from the roots to all parts of the plant.

Roots take up water and mineral salts from soil.

Sowing seeds

When a seed germinates it sprouts and grows into a young plant.

A tiny root pushes out of the seed and down into the soil. Then a shoot grows up towards the light. Leaves grow to make food and the roots spread to find water. A flower grows and is pollinated by insects. A new seed grows that will produce new plants the following year.

Scattering seeds

Some seeds just drop from the plant to the ground. Here are some plants that have more unusual ways of spreading their seeds.

In summer, gorse pods snap open in the hot sun and shoot out their seeds with a loud pop!

Sycamore and ash seeds have wings that spin like helicopter blades.

Dandelion and thistle seeds have tiny parachutes that float on the breeze.

Some flowers, such as poppies. have seed heads like pepper pots. As they sway in the wind the seeds are thrown out.

What is a flower?

The flower is very important because it produces the seeds for the new plant.

Insects are very important to the flower. As insects move from flower to flower to drink the nectar, the flower's dusty pollen sticks to them and falls on the next flower that the insect visits. This pollinates the flower to make seeds.

Petal

Stamen with pollen

Stigma

Eggs

Sepal

Fungi and Cacti

Fungi come in many different shapes and sizes. They grow as mushrooms in fields and also as fluffy grey mould on stale food.

Fungi cannot make their own food, like other plants. Instead they get a ready-made food supply by growing on other plants or decaying matter, like rotting wood or dead leaves.

Fungi have no flowers or seeds, they scatter fine spores just like the fern group of plants. Although some fungi, such as the mushroom, can be eaten, many are poisonous.

It is safer to leave them alone!

Velvet Shank

Cup Fungus

Spores

Shaggy Inkcap

Wood Agaric

Fairy Ring Mushroom

Fly Agaric

Most plants cannot survive in the hot, dry desert. There is not enough water in the soil to replace the moisture lost through their leaves.

The cactus plants are able to store water in the fleshy parts within their thick, tough skins. No water is lost through their leaves which are the prickly spikes like needles. These also protect the plant from animals seeking moisture.

Cacti produce beautiful flowers, but they do so very rarely, sometimes only once in their lifetime – just enough to produce their seeds.

Plants we eat

Much of the food we eat comes from plants. There are many different plants that are eaten all over the world.

The group of plants known as cereals are grown so that their seeds can be gathered, or harvested as grain, which is the world's main food.

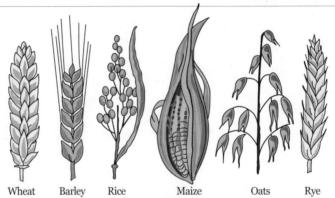

Wheat Barley Rice Maize Oats Rye

Giant Saguaro grows up to 18m (60ft) tall

Fruits contain the seeds of flowering plants. A peach has one seed, a melon has hundreds. Oranges and lemons are citrus fruits that grow on evergreen shrubs in warm lands.

Orange

Melon

Strawberry

Lemon

Apple

Peach

Lime

Grapes

Blueberries

Pear

Banana

Blackberry

Vegetables – we eat the roots of the carrot, turnip and potato; the leaves of cabbages, lettuce and broccoli, and the leaf stalks of celery, leeks and onions. Dried peas, beans and lentils are pulses, and are full of protein.

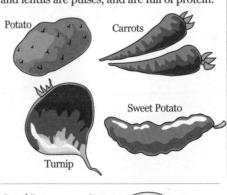

Potato

Carrots

Sweet Potato

Turnip

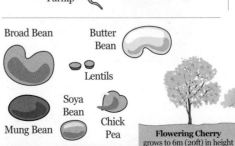

Broad Bean Butter Bean

Lentils

Soya Bean

Mung Bean Chick Pea

Cabbage

Broccoli

Lettuce

Celery

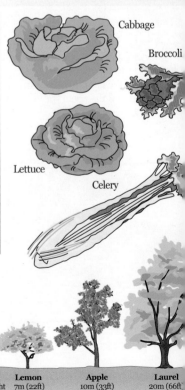

Flowering Cherry grows to 6m (20ft) in height **Lemon** 7m (22ft) **Apple** 10m (33ft) **Laurel** 20m (66ft)

14

Trees

Trees can grow larger and live longer than any other living thing on earth. The giant sequoia can reach over 100 metres (328ft) and live for over 3,000 years. It is the world's tallest tree.

A tree grows very slowly, upwards and outwards.
The roots spread out underground, some deep in the ground and others near the surface.

Deciduous trees with broad fat leaves stop growing in the cold weather. They do not need their leaves to trap sunlight or give off moisture, so they shed them as winter approaches.

Evergreen trees have tough, thin leaves like needles that lose very little water. They do not shed their leaves in winter, they stay 'ever green'.

However large the tree, it still grew from a seed just as smaller plants do.

Acorns are the seeds of the mighty oak.

Trees like pine and fir keep their seeds hidden inside beautiful cones.

The Kings Of The Forest

Each year as a tree grows, it adds a new ring of wood beneath the bark. When a tree is cut down you can find out its age by counting the rings. Imagine the history in the ring of the great sequoia, which is over 3,000 years old.

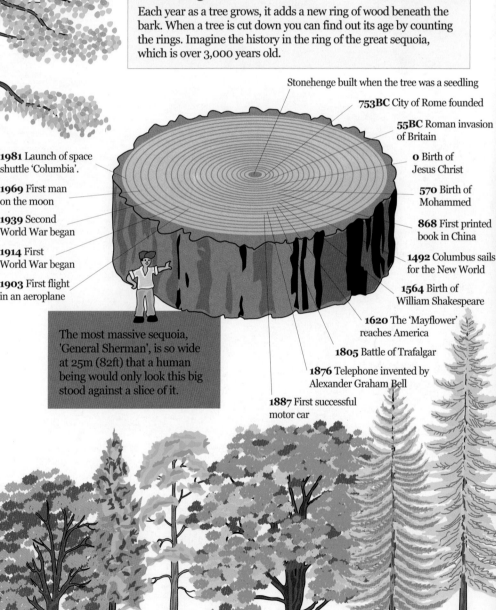

Stonehenge built when the tree was a seedling

753BC City of Rome founded

55BC Roman invasion of Britain

0 Birth of Jesus Christ

570 Birth of Mohammed

868 First printed book in China

1492 Columbus sails for the New World

1564 Birth of William Shakespeare

1620 The 'Mayflower' reaches America

1805 Battle of Trafalgar

1876 Telephone invented by Alexander Graham Bell

1887 First successful motor car

1981 Launch of space shuttle 'Columbia'.

1969 First man on the moon

1939 Second World War began

1914 First World War began

1903 First flight in an aeroplane

The most massive sequoia, 'General Sherman', is so wide at 25m (82ft) that a human being would only look this big stood against a slice of it.

Trees come in many shapes and sizes, here are some well known ones:

| Weeping Willow 22m (72ft) | Yew 22m (82ft) | Sequoia 100m (328ft) | Beech 30m (98ft) | Poplar 35m (115ft) | Scots Pine 35m (115ft) | Oak 35m (115ft) | Larch 40m (131ft) | Douglas Fir 50m+ (64ft+) |

Insects

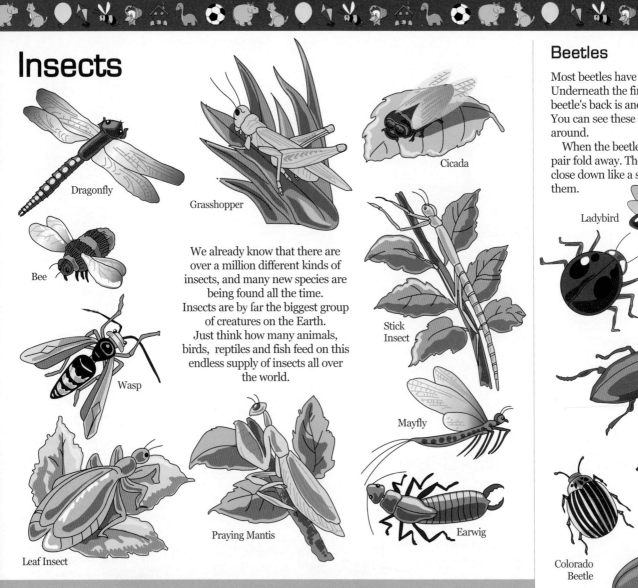

Dragonfly

Bee

Wasp

Grasshopper

Cicada

Stick Insect

Mayfly

Earwig

Leaf Insect

Praying Mantis

We already know that there are over a million different kinds of insects, and many new species are being found all the time.
Insects are by far the biggest group of creatures on the Earth.
Just think how many animals, birds, reptiles and fish feed on this endless supply of insects all over the world.

What is an insect?

An insect is a creature without a backbone and with a body divided into three main parts: the head, thorax and abdomen.

Most insects have three pairs of legs and one or two pairs of wings. The 'feelers' or antennae on the insect's head are its sense of touch and smell.

Some insects have a sting in the abdomen.

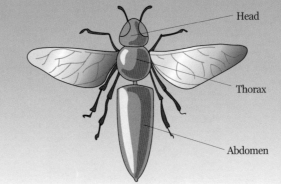

Head

Thorax

Abdomen

Ants and Termites

Ants live together in large colonies and often make nests underground. The ant hill is full of passages and separate cells for eggs and food.

Worker ants build the nests, gather food and look after the larvae that hatch from the eggs, until they turn into young ants.

Termites are ant-like insects. They build huge mounds of earth from grains of soil.

Inside live millions of termites in tunnels and chambers. Some mounds are over eight metres (26ft) high.

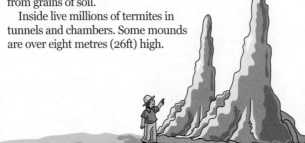

Beetles

Most beetles have two pairs of wings. Underneath the first hard pair on the beetle's back is another delicate pair. You can see these as the beetle flies around.

When the beetle lands, the second pair fold away. The first pair then close down like a shell to protect them.

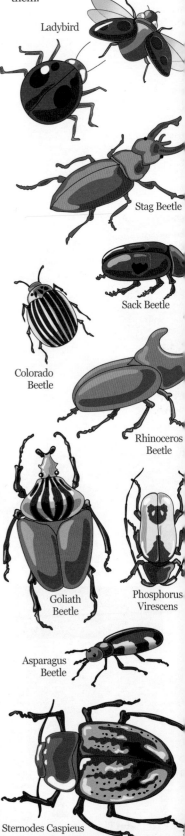

Ladybird

Stag Beetle

Sack Beetle

Colorado Beetle

Rhinoceros Beetle

Goliath Beetle

Phosphorus Virescens

Asparagus Beetle

Sternodes Caspieus

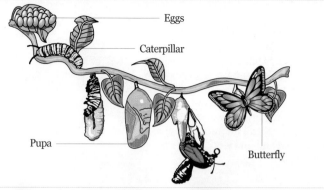

Eggs

Caterpillar

Pupa

Butterfly

Butterflies

A butterfly begins life as an egg. The egg hatches and out comes a caterpillar. The caterpillar grows, shedding its skin several times. At full size it becomes a pupa in a hard shell. After a while the shell cracks open and out squeezes a new butterfly.

Butterflies love the sunshine. If you walk in a garden on a sunny day you will often find beautiful butterflies feeding on the nectar of bright flowers and blossoms.

Their lovely colours are made up of millions of minute scales that overlap one after another and cover the wings. These can only be seen through a microscope, as they are as fine as dust. Butterflies shouldn't be picked up as this rubs off the scales, making flight difficult.

Large Blue

Monarch

Ulysses

Large Copper

Green Hairstreak resting with wings folded.

Brimstone

Small Tortoiseshell

Moths

Butterflies and moths look very much alike, but moths usually fly by night and rest by day.

When a butterfly rests, its wings are closed and held straight up, while a moth keeps its wings spread out flat.

Moths are not usually as colourful as butterflies, and their bodies have a fatter shape.

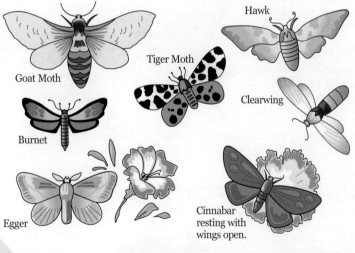

Hawk

Tiger Moth

Goat Moth

Clearwing

Burnet

Egger

Cinnabar resting with wings open.

Is a spider an insect?

Look at a spider. You will see it has eight legs and its body is divided into two parts. This means it is not an insect. It is an arachnid and belongs to the same family as the scorpion.

The spider spins a sticky, silk thread, then builds a web to catch insects. When the spider feels the web move, it knows it has caught a meal.

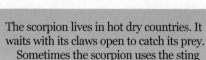

The scorpion lives in hot dry countries. It waits with its claws open to catch its prey.

Sometimes the scorpion uses the sting at the top of its tail to paralyse large insects it cannot catch with its claws.

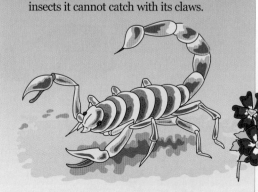

What a pest!

Some insects do a great deal of harm. They can destroy crops and spread sickness and disease. We call these insects pests!

Flies can be a danger to health – they breed in refuse and carry germs on their feet that they can transfer to any food that is uncovered.

Locusts are a type of grasshopper. In the tropics they swarm in search of food, often travelling over 1000km (621 miles). When a swarm lands, the insects eat vast quantities of crops and food, which causes famine in some lands.

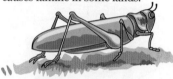

Mosquitoes can be a serious pest in tropical countries, because they spread a sickness called malaria. They feed by piercing the skin, then sucking out the blood. This infects the wound with germs and spreads the disease.

Bees

Bees do an important job for all the plant life of this planet.

As they fly from flower to flower collecting nectar, dusty pollen clings to their legs and bodies. This pollinates the flowers so that they will produce seeds.

17

Birds

Birds are warm-blooded creatures. Their bodies are covered in feathers that help to keep them warm and dry. There are over 8,600 different kinds of birds in the world. They all have wings – but not all of them can fly!

All birds lay eggs, inside which young birds develop. When a baby bird grows too big for its egg, it chips a hole in the shell from inside, and very soon hatches out.

Feathers and flight

Because birds fly, their bodies are designed to be as light as possible. Their feathers weigh very little, they have no teeth and their beaks are made of horn. Although their bones are hollow, they are strong and light.

The tiny humming bird can beat its wings at great speed. It can also hover in mid-air and even fly backwards.

Most birds have a streamlined shape that helps them to fly. Their wings are like strong arms that lift the bird into the air, then propel it along.

A bird can change the shape or angle of its wings to change course. Together with the tail, wings help the bird to steer, brake and land.

Many water birds have to run along the surface to gain speed before lifting off.

Eggs and nests

Baby birds that hatch in a nest start off life blind and featherless. They must be fed and kept warm for several weeks by their parents until they are ready to fly.

Other chicks that hatch out in nests on the ground or near water have fluffy down feathers and they are soon able to run around and find food. Some can even swim.

Down

Semi-plume

Vaned feather

An albatross uses its huge wing span to glide great distances over the ocean.

The kingfisher folds its wings and dives straight into the water to spear fish on its sharp beak.

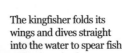

Beaks, bills and feet

The shape of a bird's beak gives us a clue about the food it eats. You can tell if a bird lives near water or on land, just by looking at its feet.

Woodcock – long beak for probing

Bullfinch – strong, sharp beak for nipping off buds

Heron – long, sharp beak for spearing fish

Hawk – sharp curved beak for tearing meat

Wren – small sharp beak for catching insects

Parrot – very strong beak for cracking nuts

Duck – broad webbed feet for swimming

Hawk – sharp hooked claws for gripping

Redshank – long wide spaced toes for wading

Partridge – short toes for walking

Finch – long, strong toes for perching

Birds that cannot fly

Of the thousands of types of birds, only a small number cannot fly. This group includes the heaviest and the largest birds – the ostrich, emu, cassowary and penguin.

Cassowary

Penguin

Takahe

Kiwi

Ostrich

Fruit and seed eaters

Parrot – eats fruit and nuts

Crossbill – picks the seed from pine cones

Quail – eats mainly grass seeds

Toucan – lives on soft fruit

Birds of Prey

These large birds catch and kill their food with their strong beaks and claws. They have very good eyesight that enables them to see any small movement on the ground.

Bald Eagle

Peregrine Falcon

Long-eared Owl

Vulture

Monkey-eating Eagle

Swimmers

Some birds are able to swim because they have slightly oily, waterproof feathers. All of the swimmers have broad, webbed feet that act like paddles. They get food such as fish, snails and plants from the water.

Herring Gull

Puffin

Canada Goose

Mute Swan

Black-necked Grebe

Teal

Insect-eaters

Most of the insect-eaters are small, fast-moving birds with sharp beaks. Some, like the swallow, catch their food in mid-air.

Bee-eater

Red-backed Shrike

Swallow

Waders

These water birds are not able to swim, they live on the water's edge. They all have long beaks and legs, and wade out into the water in search of food.

Spoonbill

Flamingo

Heron

Woodpecker

19

Life in the Seas and Oceans

There are countless numbers of creatures that make their home in the sea, from the microscopic plankton that drift near the surface, to the largest creature on Earth, the blue whale.

There are brightly coloured tropical fish that swim around the coral reefs, and strange-looking fish that live in the darkness of the ocean bed.

All are part of the endless variety of life that is found in our seas and oceans.

Bottle-nosed Dolphin

Turtle

Jellyfish

Flying Fish

Cod

Great White Shark

Killer Whale

Seal

Tuna

Mackerel

Thresher Shark

Blue Whale

Manta Ray

Giant Squid

Coelacanth

The ocean depths

The bottom of the ocean is a cold and dark place. No plants grow because there is no sunlight. There are very few fish and, because food is scarce, many have developed huge, wide-open mouths to snap up anything they come across.

Some have developed lights as lures to catch their prey.

Viperfish

Brittle Star

Deep Sea Angler

Hatched Fish

How a fish breathes

Fish breathe by taking oxygen from the water. They take the water in through their mouths and pass it over their gills, which extract the oxygen. Then the water is pushed out of the gill slits.

Swim bladder keeps the fish afloat

Dorsal fins

Tail fin

Gill silts

Stomach

Anal fin

Pelvic fin

The world's biggest fish

The biggest fish in the world is a whale shark. It is not dangerous as it lives on plankton, which is made up of tiny plants, fish eggs and larvae. This huge fish can reach 15m (50ft) in length.

Sharks belong to a very old family of fish that have skeletons of hard gristle rather than bone. Other members of this family are rays, dog fish and saw fish. They can be found in many parts of the world, but usually in tropical waters.

Most sharks feed on fish, squid or plankton, but some are ferocious, with razor sharp teeth and will eat almost anything.

Probably the most danger-ous of all is the great white, which has been known to attack and sink small boats.

Life on a coral reef

Coral is a type of chalky rock. It is made up of the hard skeletons and the living bodies of millions of tiny coral animals that live in warm shallow tropical seas. Coral exists in many different shapes and colours.

After many years the corals knit together to form huge ridges or reefs. The Great Barrier Reef off the coast of Australia is 2,000 km (1,250 miles) long. Sometimes the coral builds up to form islands and circular reefs called atolls. A coral reef is home to countless beautiful and unusual fish and plants.

Wreckfish

Emperor Angelfish

Batfish

Clown Triggerfish

Moorish Idol

Cowfish

Chocolate Clownfish

Fairy Basset

Parrotfish

The hammerhead shark, 4.2m (14ft), can be dangerous to humans.

At 8m (26ft) in length the great white shark is dwarfed by the huge whale shark.

The megamouth shark, 4.5m (15ft), is a harmless filter feeder like the whale shark.

The tiger shark is 7.4m (24ft) and dangerous to humans.

21

Amphibians

Amphibians begin their life in water. At first they breathe through gills, then their lungs develop, enabling them to live on land. They must return to the water to breed.

Frogs lay many eggs in water. Tadpoles hatch and, after a while, they grow legs and lungs. The last stage is to shed their tails before they become frogs.

Salamander

Spawn

2-3 days

3 weeks

9-10 weeks
(begins to take air)

10-12 weeks

Toad

Newt

Reptiles

In prehistoric times there were great numbers of strange reptiles, but most of them are extinct now.

The reptiles we know today include snakes, crocodiles and alligators, tortoises and turtles, and lizards. They are cold-blooded and produce their young from eggs. Their skins are usually scaly.

The turtle has flippers and lives in the sea. It is related to the tortoise, which lives on land.

European Tortoise

The Giant Tortoise of the Galapagos Islands can live over 100 years.

Green Turtles swim in the warm seas around Australia.

The Giant Leatherback Turtle of the Pacific Ocean is over 2m (6ft 6in).

Lizards

Most lizards live in warm, sunny places, and often in hot deserts.

Lizards bask in the sun to raise their body temperature. When they are warm enough they can move about quickly to search for food. As their body temperature drops, lizards slow down.

The Gila monster has a poisonous bite.

Crocodiles and Alligators

These reptiles usually live in lakes and rivers of hot countries, but they crawl up onto the bank to bask in the sunshine. They feed on fish and often grab larger animals, which they tear apart and eat in the water.

Baby crocodile breaking out of the egg.

The Chameleon can change colour slightly to blend into the background.

Iguana
S. America

The Slow Worm looks like a snake but is a legless lizard.

The Komodo Dragon of Indonesia can grow to 3m (10 ft) in length.

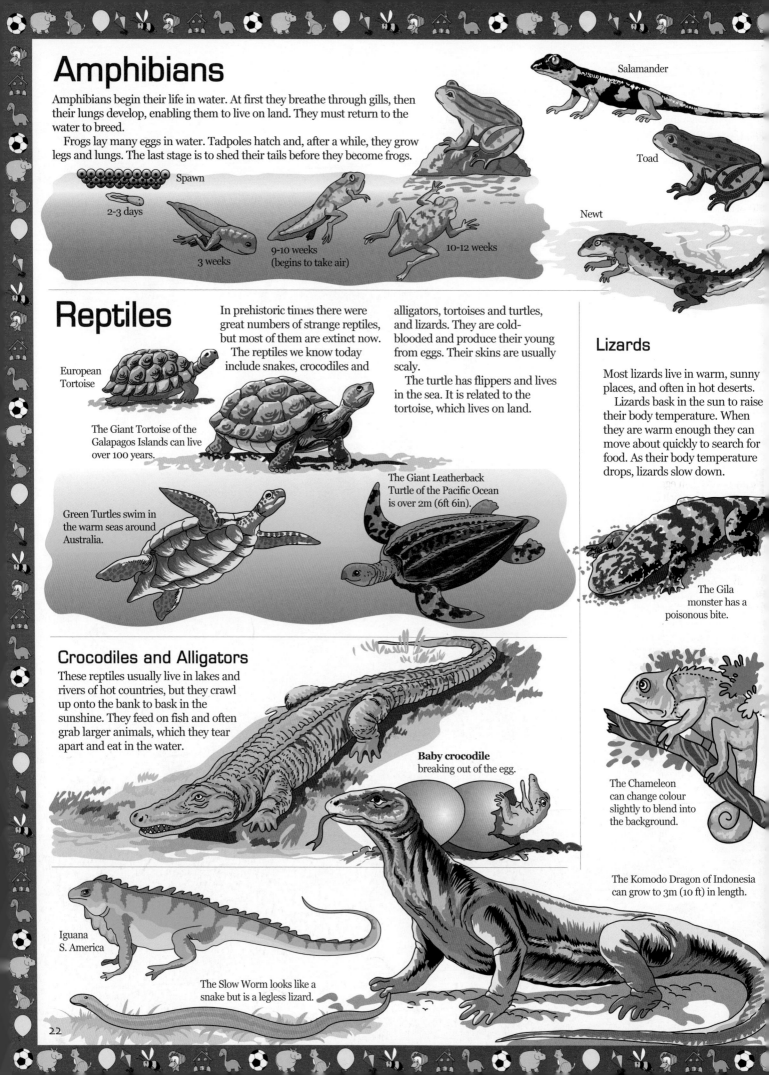

Snakes

Snakes are limbless reptiles that can vary a great deal in size and colour, but very little in shape. A snake can shed its scaly skin completely as it grows.

Many snakes are harmless, but others such as the cobra and rattlesnake kill their prey with venom.

Snakes do not chew their food, but swallow it whole. The lower jaw is in two halves and can stretch sideways so the snake can swallow larger animals than itself.

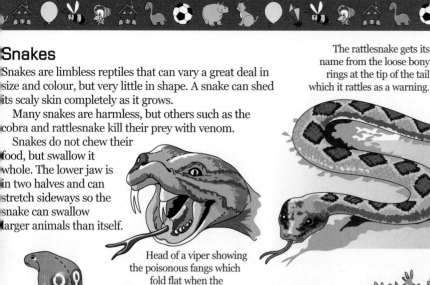

The rattlesnake gets its name from the loose bony rings at the tip of the tail which it rattles as a warning.

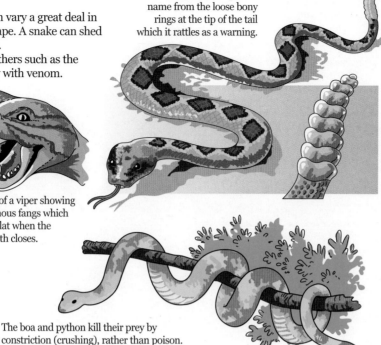

Head of a viper showing the poisonous fangs which fold flat when the mouth closes.

King Cobra

The boa and python kill their prey by constriction (crushing), rather than poison. These snakes wrap themselves around their prey, usually a small animal or bird, and squeeze.

The largest of the boas is the anaconda of S. America, which can be over 6m (20ft) in length.

The body of the sea snake is flattened for swimming. It lives in the warm Indian and Pacific Oceans and eats fish and eels. The world's most poisonous sea snake lives off the northern coast of Australia.

Mammals

Mammals are warm-blooded creatures. All of them have backbones, and some grow hair or fur on their bodies to keep warm. They feed their young on milk produced by the mother.

Humans are mammals – our babies, like all other mammals, are born as living creatures. However, there are two animals found in Australia that are the exception. They are the only egg-laying mammals in the world!

Platypus

This strange animal is part-reptile and part-mammal, with a duck-bill and webbed feet. The female platypus lays her eggs in a nest at the end of a long burrow. She hatches them with her warm furry body, then feeds her young with her milk.

Echidna

This animal is also known as the spiny anteater. It has a coat of sharp spines, a long beak and a sticky tongue. This is used to reach into the nests of termites and ants for food. The female echidna has a pouch in which she puts her eggs. Then she feeds her young with milk when they hatch.

Animals with pouches

Koala

Brush-tail Possom

Wombat

Honey Possom

Kangaroo

A world of difference

There are around 4,500 types of mammal and they behave in their own special way, and have their own unique lifestyle. Some mammals live in trees, many underground, while others live in the sea. Some can run very fast, others move slowly. Several can glide, but only one mammal – the bat – can fly. To survive, every mammal must find food, escape from danger and bring up its young.

Bats live in groups that hunt by night, while by day they hang upside-down to rest. Most bats eat insects that they find by a kind of bat radar. A bat sends out high-pitched squeaks as it flies. This wave of sound travels in front of the bat. When it hits anything in its path the sound wave bounces back rather like an echo and this is picked up by the bat's sensitive ears. Others eat fruit and a few feed on blood.

Mammals that live in the sea

Although whales, dolphins and porpoises live in the sea, they are mammals rather than fish. Mammals must have air, and all these sea creatures come to the surface to breathe.

Seals and sea lions are sea creatures that spend time on land but never move far from the seashore. Baby seals are born on the land. Seals are mainly fish eaters, but the big leopard seal eats birds too.

Furry gliders

These mammals glide from one tree to another. As they jump, they stretch out all four legs. They have flaps of skin on either side of their body that they spread out to form a type of parachute.

When gliding, the tail is used as a rudder to steer.

Australian Sugar Glider

European Flying Squirrel

Narwhal (Toothed)

Right Whale (Baleen)

Sperm Whale (Toothed)

Sea Lion (California)

Leopard Seal (Antartica)

Harp Seal and baby (Arctic)

Walrus (Arctic)

Some whales, such as the sperm whale, the narwhal, porpoises and dolphins, have teeth and feed on fish and squid.

Others like the bowhead, the blue whale and the fin whale have no teeth. They feed on tiny sea creatures by straining the water through strips of whalebone, called baleen, that hang like shelves in their mouths.

24

Grazing animals

Many mammals are plant eaters. Some graze on grass while others are tall with long necks or trunks that are perfect for reaching leaves high up in the trees.

In Africa, great areas of grassland are home to a huge variety of mammals. Some live together in great herds, often travelling long distances together in search of food and water.

They must always be on the look-out for predators. Predators are the meat-eating animals that hunt the grazing animals and kill them for food.

Elephants like to eat the highest leaves, but cause a lot of damage to the tree.

Thomson's Gazelle
This pretty little animal eats young grass shoots.

The Giraffe eats the leaves from the highest part of the tree.

The Gerenuk reaches high in the tree by standing on its hind legs.

Zebras eat the coarser grasses and stalks.

The White Rhino eats coarse grass and plants.

The Wildebeest eats the tops of sweet grasses, the herd is always on the move.

Kudu
This large antelope eats the lower leaves of the acacia tree.

able Antelope
his handsome animal with great urved horns is a grass eater.

Impala
Another of the grass eating antelopes of the African plains.

The Predators

The Lion is the greatest of the predators in Africa. It is the female that usually makes the kill.

The Hyena is quite capable of killing, but normally it just steals or scavenges.

The Leopard
This big cat likes to lie in trees and leap onto its prey.

Cape Dog, a fierce long-legged dog that can run for hours in packs.

Cheetah
The world's fastest animal uses its great speed, 113kph (70mph), to catch small antelope.

25

Monkeys and apes

Monkeys belong to the group of mammals called primates which includes apes and humans. They live mostly in trees and are found in tropical and subtropical countries.

The monkeys of S. America (the new world) are different from their cousins in Africa and Asia (the old world) as they have prehensile tails, that is, tails that can grip like a third hand.

Most monkeys are harmless, many small types such as the marmosets can be kept as pets. One group that are not very friendly are the baboons. Large and dog-like, they can be very dangerous. The mandrill is one of these.

The new world

'Monkeys of the new world (the Americas) have 'prehensile' tails, which means they can grip like an extra limb.

Howler Monkey

Lion Tamarin

Capuchin

The old world

Mandrill – African rainforest

Red Colobus – Africa

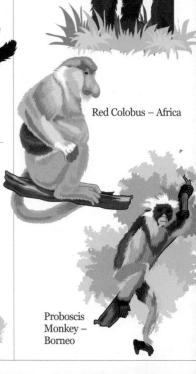

Proboscis Monkey – Borneo

The Great Apes

These are our nearest relatives in the animal world. They are the gibbon and orangutan of Borneo and Sumatra, and the chimpanzee and gorilla of Africa. None have tails.

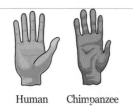

Human   Chimpanzee

Mountain Gorilla – Africa

Chimpanzee

Early Humans

It is possible that ape-like creatures living over 10 million years ago were human beings' early ancestors. Over millions of years they began to look more like us, they could make fire and use simple tools.

The first true humans appeared about 2 million years ago. Scientists called them Homo Habilis or 'Handy Man' because they could make stone tools.

About 35,000 years ago the 'Cro Magnon' race appeared. They were the ancestors of modern humans. This race probably killed off the earlier Neanderthal race.

Homo Erectus making a hand axe.

The Cro Magnon race painted beautiful pictures of animals in their caves. Perhaps they believed this would help them when hunting.

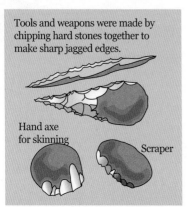

Tools and weapons were made by chipping hard stones together to make sharp jagged edges.

Hand axe for skinning

Scraper

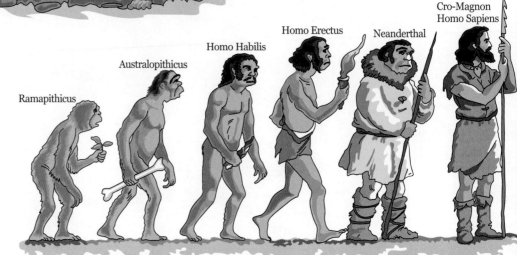

Ramapithicus

Australopithicus

Homo Habilis

Homo Erectus

Neanderthal

Cro-Magnon Homo Sapiens

Back in Time

Early human beings were hunters. To keep warm they wrapped themselves in the fur of the animals they killed. At first they made their homes in caves or they lived in simple shelters made from branches and animal skins.

When early humans learned how to grow crops, and keep cattle and sheep, they had to settle in one place and build a home.

Gradually, people learned to spin wool from their sheep and weave it into cloth. They began to use baskets and pots, and they made tools and ornaments from bronze and iron.

People built their homes in groups to feel safe. A few houses grew into a village, then a town, which in turn became a city.

The Romans

The Romans were great soldiers. Their armies marched on foot from Italy, into Europe and North Africa. In the lands they conquered they built fine roads, bridges and forts. They founded great cities. You can see the remains of some of their buildings today.

They wore tunics or gowns with a toga on top. The houses of wealthy Romans were very grand, with mosaic floors and pictures painted on the walls. Some houses had under-floor heating, and the public baths had hot pools and steam rooms.

The Egyptians

The kings and queens of Egypt were buried in huge stone pyramids built in the desert. These royal tombs held rooms full of treasure, gold, jewellery, clothes and furniture – for use in the 'afterlife'.

The Egyptians wore loose clothes made of linen to keep cool. They used make-up, perfume and wore long wigs and fancy headdresses.

The Greeks

The Greeks built beautiful temples to their gods. They were great architects and sculptors. They also loved the theatre. Their plays and poems are still read today.

The ancient Greeks began the Olympic Games. This was a sports contest held every four years in Olympia. Chariot races, running, long jumps, discus, javelin, boxing and wrestling were all part of the first Olympic Games.

The Vikings

The Vikings were sea-pirates who raided the coasts of Britain and Europe. They were fierce fighters armed with wooden shields, heavy swords and battle axes. They came from the cold climate of Northern Europe and wore woollen shirts and pants, heavy cloaks and fur-lined leather boots. The women wore bronze and silver brooches on their clothes.

The Normans

At first the Normans built wooden castles in the middle of a strong stockade. Later, they built castles of solid stone, often surrounded by a water-filled moat. To enter the castle you had to cross a drawbridge. Some castles were so big they looked like small towns. In times of danger the people would retreat inside the castle walls for safety.

The Middle Ages

In the Middle Ages all land was owned by a king. A knight gave his services and fought for his king in return for lands and sometimes a castle.

Knights wore chain mail and armour to protect themselves from the swords and arrows of the enemy. Kings, knights and noblemen all had different coats-of-arms or emblems on their flags and shields. They were known by these emblems and could be recognised on the battlefield.

Nobleman

Knight

Jesters were musicians and clowns – their job was to amuse the lords and ladies.

Peasant

Lady

The Renaissance

This was a time of new thinking and learning. Ideas quickly spread from Italy across Europe because of the invention of printing. Now people could learn about the latest discoveries in astrology and other sciences.

Explorers sailed away to find new countries and make maps of their voyages. It was also a time for great artists, sculptors and architects.

The scientist Galileo built a telescope to study the stars and planets. He believed, correctly, that the Earth moved and revolved around the Sun, and was not the centre of the universe, as people had thought in the past.

The Elizabethans

In Queen Elizabeth's reign, the costumes of the wealthy class were richly embroidered and covered in jewels. Men and women wore starched ruffs round their necks and padding in their clothes.

The Elizabethan seamen were daring adventurers. Sir Francis Drake sailed around the world in the Golden Hind. Sir Walter Raleigh led expeditions of discovery and he named the state of Virginia in America after the Queen. Raleigh also brought the first potatoes back to England.

The Pilgrim Fathers

Over 100 people left England in 1620 and sailed for America, because they were not allowed to worship as they wanted.

After 66 days at sea in the Mayflower, they stepped ashore at Cape Cod, Massachusetts.

A long hard year followed in which many of them died. In spite of this they harvested their first crops and built new homes. They had so much food they celebrated the first Thanksgiving with their new found Indian friends.

Georgian Times

In Georgian times fashion became very important. Wealthy people dressed in elegant clothes and cared a lot about the way they looked.

Even children had their own style of clothes and were not dressed like grown-ups, as they had been in the past.

Rich landowners built fine mansions, often taking away the land of the country people. This meant that the villagers had to work for the landowners for a very small wage and often had to leave their homes.

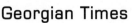

William Shakespeare 1564-1616
He wrote plays and often acted in them in his own theatre, the Globe. His plays have been translated into many languages all over the world.

The Industrial Revolution

This was the age of machines, factories, mills and mines. Spinning and weaving cloth had been done by people in their homes. Now this work could be done much quicker by machines driven by steam engines.

Country people were forced to move into towns and toil in the factories. There, adults and children worked long hours and lived in dirty, crowded slums.

By the end of the 19th century a few caring people worked hard to improve these terrible conditions by passing new laws.

People Around the World

There are around 6 billion people in the world. All have very different customs and beliefs, speak many different languages and live in very different ways.

Originally everyone belonged to one of three main groups: Caucasoid, Mongoloid and Negroid.

Thousands of years ago, the races could not mix. They did not travel from country to country as we do. They were unable to cross great distances. Today, it is easy for different races to meet, mix and live together, because travel is much quicker and easier.

N. American Indian

N. America

Eskimo

Britain

Scandinavia

Russia

China

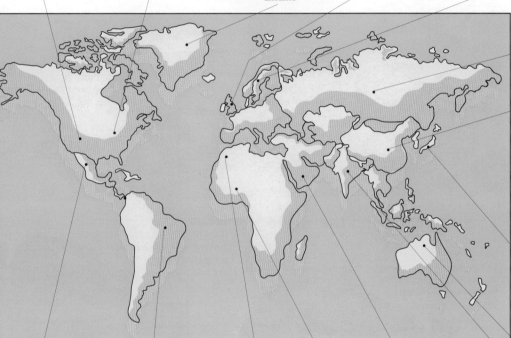

Japan

Mexico

Brazil

N. Africa

Africa

Arabia

India

Aborigine

Caucasoid

The Caucasoid people originate in Europe, the Middle East and India. The colour of their skin varies from pale in cool, cloudy climates to olive brown in warm climates.

Mongoloid

This group makes up about 3/4 of the world's population. It includes people who live in South-East and Central Asia, Mongolia, Tibet, American Indians and Eskimos. Their hair is black and straight. They have an extra fold of skin on their upper eyelids.

Negroid

These people have dark brown to black skin. This helps protect them from the rays of the hot sun, as the Negroid people originate from Africa. Their hair is black and tightly curled.

Food

Food contains nutrients that we all need to keep us alive and healthy. It helps us to grow, gives us energy, keeps our bodies warm and helps us to fight infection.

It is important for us to have a well-balanced diet. We should eat a combination of food that contains some proteins, carbohydrates, fats, vitamins and minerals.

Why food is cooked

When food is cooked, the heat kills harmful germs. Cooked food is easier for us to digest. It also keeps longer and some food tastes nicer cooked.

Fry
Cooking in hot oil or fat.

Microwave
This special oven cooks food very fast in seconds and minutes instead of hours.

Bake or roast
Cooking in an oven full of hot air. You can also roast on a spit over flames.

Boil or stew
Cooking in liquid in a pan.

Steam
Cooking in the steam that rises from boiling water.

Grill
Cooking underneath the heat, or barbecuing over a fire.

Proteins

These help to build a strong and healthy body.

Fats

Our body stores up fat to use as energy and protect us from the cold.

Carbohydrates

These starchy foods give us energy and warmth.

Vitamins and minerals

We only need very small amounts of vitamins and minerals every day to keep us healthy.

How people eat their food

In Europe main meals are eaten with a knife and fork.

In the USA food is often cut up first and then eaten with a fork.

Japanese and Chinese food is chopped before cooking and eaten with chopsticks.

In India meals are eaten with the fingers. In the Middle East just the right hand is used.

Food from around the world

Sweden
The Swedes eat smorgasbord – open sandwiches that may have smoked or pickled herrings on top.

Italy
Pizza – with a crisp base and different toppings, and spaghetti – one of the many different shaped pastas.

Japan
Each dish is beautiful to look at. Sushi is raw fish and rice made into pretty shapes.

Mexico
Food from Mexico is hot and spicy. Meat and beans are cooked with hot chillies. Tortillas are a thick maize pancake.

Britain
Roast beef, served with Yorkshire pudding cooked in the meat juices.

USA
Hamburgers and fries are very popular here.

India
Meat and vegetable curries, a lentil dish called daal, and chapatties.

China
Soup, rice and noodles are served in little bowls. Everyone helps themselves with chopsticks.

Turkey
Kebabs – meat and vegetables cooked on skewers, with pitta bread that opens into a pocket.

Your Body

The human body is like a super machine, with hundreds of moving parts and miles of tubes. The control centre of the body is the brain.

The brain stores all our learning, controls all that we see, hear and think, and every little movement we make, even while we are sleeping. Here are some of the main parts of your body.

Your stomach

The stomach churns up everything we eat into a soup. Some salts, water and sugar are absorbed into the blood. The soup passes into the small intestine, a 7m (23ft) long tube. Valuable proteins and sugars go to the liver for storage. Unwanted liquids go through the kidneys to the bladder and out of the body. In the large intestine, water is removed and the remaining waste passes out of the body.

Your heart

The heart is a muscle that pumps blood around the body every minute of the day. An adult man has 5-6 litres of blood – the heart pumps most of this every minute, but it can pump 20 litres a minute if the man is running fast.

Large Intestine

Small Intestine

Skull

Jaw Bone

Collar Bone

Shoulder Blade

Humerus

Breast Bone

Radius

Rib

Ulna

Back Bone

Your lungs

The lungs are spongy, air-filled organs that take in the air we breathe and supply oxygen to the blood which passes through them. They remove the carbon dioxide from the blood and then breathe it out again. They keep your blood rich in oxygen.

Femur

Pelvis

Knee Cap

Your liver and kidneys

The liver is a very large organ that is vital to our health because it processes and stores the goodness from our food. It also removes old cells from the blood.

The two kidneys, although small, are also vital because they purify our whole bloodstream every hour throughout the day.

Tibia

Fibula

Your skeleton

The skeleton is the framework of bones that holds us together. There are 206 bones in the adult body. They support our muscles and protect the important organs such as the heart and lungs within the rib cage.

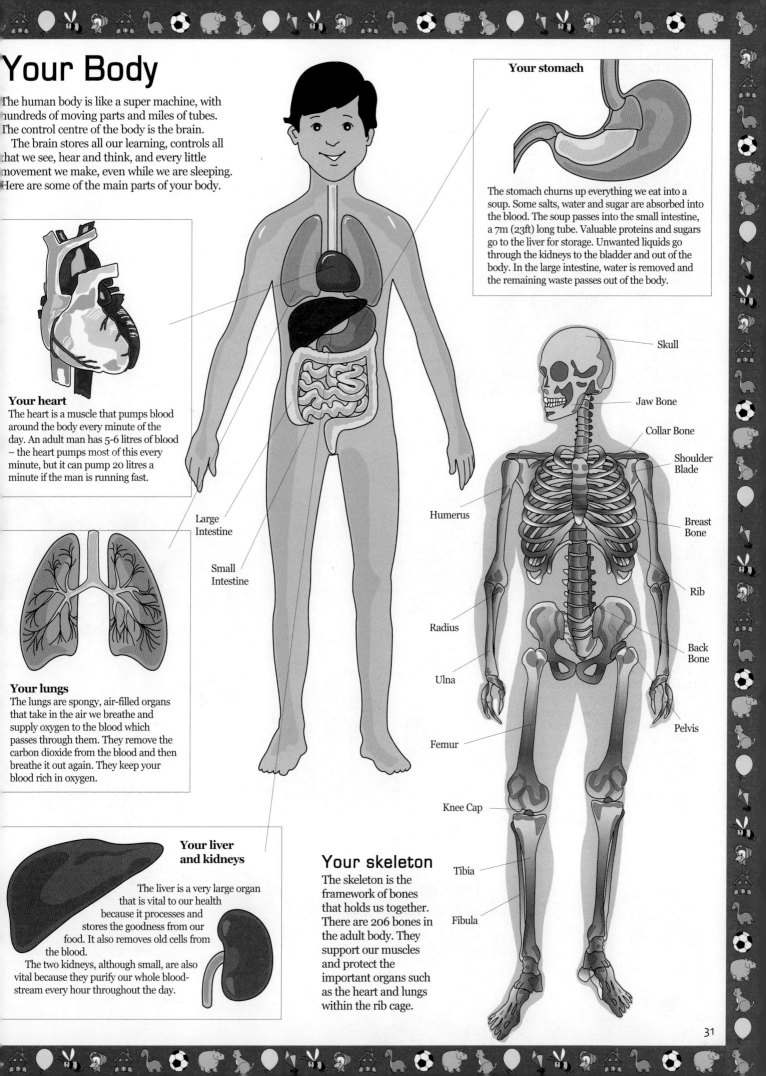

Muscles and joints

If we didn't have muscles we wouldn't be able to move. We need almost 200 muscles to take just one step. There are over 650 muscles in our bodies giving us the strength to lift heavy objects or control the most delicate movements.

The muscles work by pulling (never pushing) on the bones of the skeleton to which they are attached.

Joints are like hinges that join bones together and allow bending, twisting movements. The shoulder and hip joints have the best range of movements.

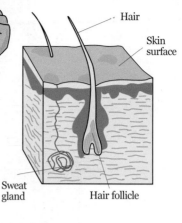

Triceps

Biceps

When we want to raise our forearm, the biceps muscle at the front of the arm contracts and shortens. This pulls the arm up. To lower the arm, the triceps muscle at the back of the arm contracts and pulls the arm down again.

Pelvis

Fluid

Femur

The hip joint
This is a ball and socket joint. The bones have a tough covering surrounded by fluid to stop them rubbing together.

Skin, hair and teeth

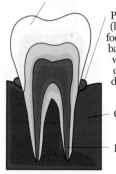

Hair

Skin surface

Sweat gland

Hair follicle

Skin is a waterpro covering over our body. helps to keep harmful germ out and to regulate our bod temperature. When the bod is hot the skin sweats an the blood vessels expan Hair grows from the sk at about 12mm (1/2 inch) month and each hair liv for about three years, then new one grow

Teeth grow from the top and bottom jawbones. We are born without teeth – young children have 20 milk teeth that are slowly replaced around the age of six until we have a full set of 32. These must be kept clean with regular brushing.

Hard enamel cover

Plaque (bits o food an bacteri which cause decay)

Gum

Root

The wonderful brain

The human brain is like a super computer. It stores millions of bits of information that it can recall instantly. We record all the information that our senses gather. This is how we recognise a friend out of all the thousands of people we have seen, or a sound that we have heard maybe years before.

At the same time as it is collecting information from you watching TV or reading a book, the brain is controlling all the thousands of tiny things that are going on in your body – yet this wonderful little creation weighs only about 1.4kg (3lb).

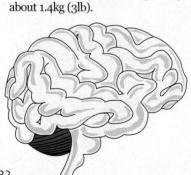

The senses

Everyone should have five senses, each one giving us important information. We see with our eyes, hear with our ears, taste with our tongue, smell with our nose and feel through our skin.

Cornea

Iris

Pupil

Lens

Retina

Optic nerve to brain

The eye

The human eye is round like a ball. The outer layer is a tough white coat that is clear at the front. Light passes through this, through the pupil and the lens. It then strikes the retina at the back. This tells the brain what it sees.

The ear

Sound is a vibration in the air that travels in waves. These waves strike the eardrum, which passes the sound through nerves to the brain, which recognises the sound and tells us what we have heard.

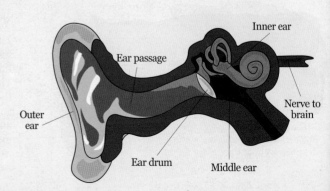

Inner ear

Ear passage

Outer ear

Nerve to brain

Ear drum

Middle ear

Transport

When early humans moved from place to place they had to walk. If they needed to move something, they had to carry it. Heavy loads were dragged on sledges, and animals, usually oxen, were used to help. If the load was very heavy it was placed on rollers made from tree trunks. This was a very slow job until, about 5,000 years ago, the wheel was invented.

The first wheel was probably just a slice of log. This would soon crack and split. A wheel made of several pieces would be stronger, but very heavy. It was a long before the spoked wheel was invented. This meant that wheels could be strong, but lighter.

For hundreds of years people travelled by wagon, and carried trade goods in heavy carts. It must have been very slow and uncomfortable, especially as roads were just muddy, stoney tracks.

The Greeks and Romans used the spoked wheel with a metal rim for their chariots. These were light, fast, two-wheeled carriages. They would often have races.

From the 17th until the 19th century, when the railways were built, people travelled long distances by coach. These were drawn by four or six horses that were changed often at special stopping places called stages.

the Locomotion

The steam train

The first public railway in the world opened in 1825. It ran between Stockton andDarlington in England. Thirty-four wagons carrying coal or passengers were pulled by the steam engine (called the 'locomotion'). This engine was designed by George Stephenson who then built the famous 'Rocket' that ran from Manchester to Liverpool in 1830. He won a prize of £500 for the Rocket in 1829.

Steam transport had begun and soon spread into Europe and America.

The motor car

The big change in road transport began when a German engineer, Karl-Friedrich Benz, produced the world's first petrol-driven motor car in 1885. He then joined forces with Gottlieb Daimler to pioneer the high-speed T-stroke petrol engine.

The early cars were called 'horseless carriages' because they still looked like carriages. They were slow and open to the weather, and both driver and passengers wore long coats and goggles for protection.

an early motor car

Modern Trains

From the early days of the Locomotion and Rocket the steam engine grew in speed, size and power. Huge engines pulled trade goods and passengers across continents. In some parts of China, India and Africa these original great steam engines are still hard at work. The fastest steam train ever was the 'Mallard' or British engine, which reached 201 kph (125mph) in 1938.

Diesel trains

Diesels had replaced steam engines by the 1950s. These ran on diesel fuel instead of coal and were therefore much cleaner.

The diesel speed record is 238.9 kph (148.5mph), set in 1987.

Electric trains

Trains driven by electricity are clean, quiet and fast. A frame called a 'pantograph' on top of the train is in contact with the power cable all the time the train is running. This French TGV train travels at a speed of 270kph (168mph) but can exceed 300 kph (186mph).

The bullet train

The famous bullet trains have been in service in Japan since 1964. Speeding along at 210 kph (130mph) these trains carry almost half a million passengers a day on the 512km (320 mile) line between Tokyo and Osaka.

Future trains

Different ideas for the future are currently being developed. One that is already working is 'maglev' (magnetic levitation). Magnets make the train hover 15mm (5/8 inches) above a special track. The train has no wheels, no moving parts, and is almost silent when running. In 1987 in Japan, a maglev test train carried passengers at 400 kph (249 mph).

1 Linear motor for forward movement and braking
2 Reaction rails
3 Suspension rails
4 Electromagnets lift the train

Bikes

The bike is a very useful machine and can be great fun.

The first true pedal bicycle was the hobby horse, invented in 1839. It was very heavy, with iron rims around the wheels.

Modern bicycles are made from light alloy tubes and are very strong and fast.

1861 – the first fro wheel pedalled bik

34

The Car

Early cars were very expensive because they were hand-built by craftsmen, using expensive materials.

An American named Henry Ford changed this by building a car that everyone could own. In 1908 he designed the Ford model T and, more importantly, the world's first assembly line to mass produce the car. By 1927 over 15,000,000 of these had been sold.

This is a sports car, it is very fast to drive.

This is a four-wheel drive vehicle. In most cars the engine drives only two wheels, usually the back. In this vehicle all four wheels are driven – this gives a much better grip on rough or slippery ground.

This is a truck. It carries large amounts of goods to shops and factories. It has a very big powerful engine that runs on diesel fuel, not petrol.

Modern BMX bikes are very strong and can be ridden over rough ground.

The motor bike is a high speed two-wheeled machine. It needs skill and training to handle properly.

The Engine

The car engine has four or more tubes called cylinders. In each cylinder is a piston that goes up and down and turns the crankshaft that drives the wheels.

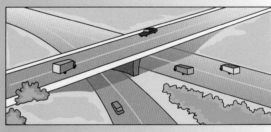

A - Cylinder   B - Piston   C - Exhaust valve   D - Inlet valve   E - Crankshaft   F - Spark plug

1 The piston goes down and sucks in petrol mixed with air

2 The piston goes up again and squeezes the mixture into a small space

3 The spark plug causes an explosion that pushes the piston down

4 The piston goes up and pushes burnt gases out of the cylinders

All of this happens at great speed while the engine is running.

Roads and Bridges

The Romans built the first roads, which were long, straight and made of stones set in mortar.

Modern roads are made of concrete surfaced with small stones and covered in tar.

Bridge-building meant that fast traffic could 'fly over' other roads without stopping. Bridges also carry railway lines over valleys or rivers.

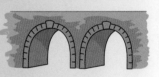

The type of bridge used depends on the span (width) and the weight it has to carry. The Romans discovered the strength of the arched bridge, a design still used today.

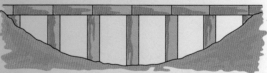

Beam bridge

Arch bridge

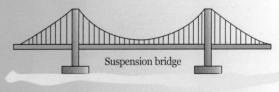

Suspension bridge

Cantilever

Ships and Boats

Canoe
Made from skin stretched over a wooden frame.

Egyptian boat
The earliest sailboat. The two large oars at the back were for steering. Similar boats can still be seen on the Nile.

Greek Galley
These large, fast ships were rowed by slaves. The point underwater was for ramming.

Viking Longship
The vikings sailed great distances in their shallow bottomed ships, even to North America.

Arab Dhow
This ancient craft is still in everyday use in the Middle East.

Chinese Junk
Another craft still in use after thousands of years.

Early humans first crossed water by sitting astride logs and paddling. Later they made rafts by lashing logs together. Then they hollowed out logs to make a canoe. To make their craft lighter they stretched animal skins over a wooden frame.

The ancient Egyptians first used ships with a sail on the River Nile about 5,000 years ago.

Over the centuries ships got bigger, with multiple masts and sails.

Why does a ship float?
How can a huge ship made of metal float on water? A ship is hollow, and when it's in water it pushes the water out of the way. This principle is called 'displacement', discovered by the ancient Greek scientist, Archimedes.

The weight of the ship pushes down into the water but the water pushes back with equal force.

Try this at home: place an empty plastic bowl in a sinkful of water – the bowl will float like a ship. Press the bowl downwards – the harder you push, the more the water will push back to keep the bowl afloat.

The Mayflower
Some ships have become as famous in history as the men and women who sailed in them. The Mayflower was the little ship that carried the Pilgrim Fathers across the Atlantic ocean to America in 1620. They were seeking the freedom to practise their religion in safety.

The Clippers
In the mid 1800s there was a great need for fast ships to carry cargo around the world, and so the 'clipper' was designed. They were often called 'tea clippers' because they would race from China with a cargo of tea for the merchants of Britain and America.

Sail and steam
The first steamships still had sails for extra power. This ship is the Great Britain, launched in 1845. It was the first iron-hulled ocean-going ship, and the first propeller ship to cross the Atlantic Ocean.

The Plimsoll line
This marks the depth to which a ship can be safely loaded. It was suggested by British MP Samuel Plimsoll in 1876, to regulate trade shipping inspection. It varies with the time of year and the kind of water.

TF
F
T
L   R   S
W
WNA

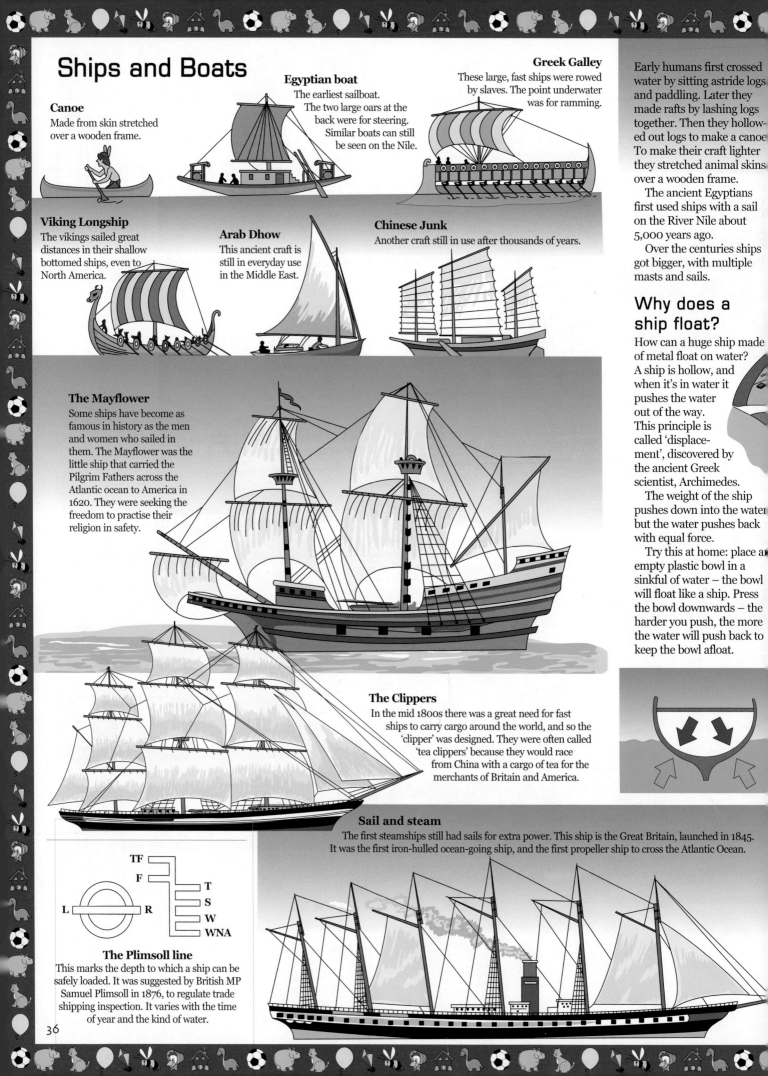

Modern ships and boats

There are many types of ship today, from the giant oil tankers to the little tugs that pull them around. All are designed for a particular job.

Hydrofoils

The hydrofoil looks like an ordinary boat, but below the water it has wings. As it speeds up, the wings provide 'lift', just like an aircraft's wings and the boat rises out of the water. This reduces the drag that slows a conventional ship down.

Fishing boats

Fishing boats come in all shapes and sizes. The largest are like floating factories, they catch, clean and freeze the fish without having to return to harbour.

Oil Tankers

These are the largest ships in the world. The biggest is 458m (1,504ft) in length and is called the 'Seawise Giant'. On some tankers the crew use bicycles to move around on deck. These ocean giants deliver oil all round the world. Because of their size they cannot go into port, instead they unload onto smaller ships or jetties built out into deep water.

Car ferry

These amazing ships carry cars, lorries or coaches with all their passengers. The vehicles drive in at one end, and out at the other when they reach their destination.

Submarines

These are underwater boats. They have large air tanks down each side. The boat floats when It is full of air and submerges when water is flooded into the air tanks.

Tugs

The tug is a small but very powerful motor boat. It tows or pushes large ships in small spaces, or helps to recover damaged ships.

Cargo ships

These ships carry all kinds of trade goods around the world. They have their own cranes on deck so they can load or unload themselves.

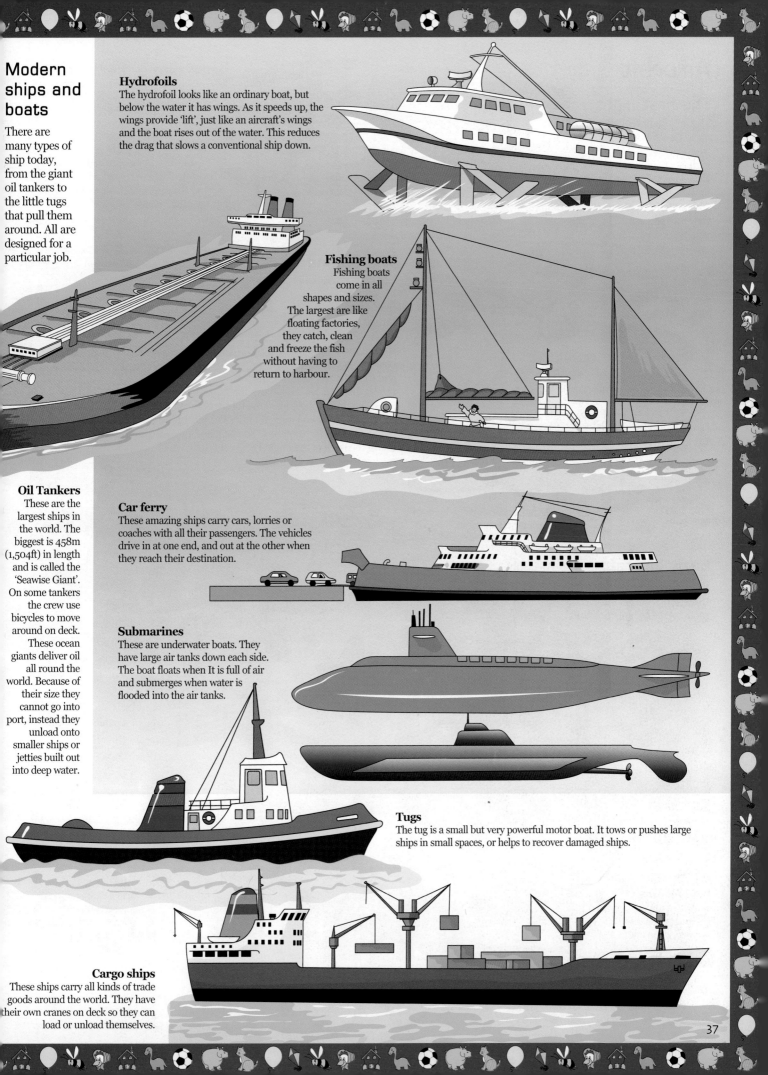

Aircraft

The first flight

The first flight took place on 17 December 1903, when Wilbur and Orville Wright took off from Kitty Hawk, North Carolina, in the United States of America. Although they only ascended 260m (852 ft), they proved air travel was possible.

How can a machine fly?

The answer is the engine that pushes the aircraft forward, and the shape of the wing that gives 'lift'.

If you cut through a wing, the shape would be like this picture. The curve on the top of the wing makes the air travel fast over it. This lowers the pressure of the air and the stronger pressure under the wing pushes upwards, giving 'lift'.

Lift

Air is sucked in and compressed.

Burning fuel heats the air, which drives the turbine

The air is reheated.

The engine

The early aircraft all had 'piston' engines (like a car) which turned a propeller. When a propeller spins it pushes the air backwards very fast, and the aircraft moves forward.

The engine that changed the future of flying was the jet, first invented in 1930 by British engineer Frank Whittle. The jet engine sucks in air that it compresses and heats with burning fuel. The heat and pressure force gases out of the back of the engine at great speed, which pushes the aircraft forward.

compressor

The turbine drives the compressor which sucks in more air.

Early aircraft

Early aircraft had wooden frames covered with fabric. They needed two or three wings to give lift. As engine wing design improved, the single winged metal plane became possible.

Fokker Triplane (3 wings)

Hawker Biplane (2 wings)

Spitfire Monoplane (single wing)

How an aircraft manoeuvres

Aircraft have moveable parts on the wings and tail. The pilot uses these to control the movements of the aircraft in the air.

Ailerons
The ailerons are used with the rudder to bank the aircraft into a turn.

Rudder
The rudder turns the aircraft to the left or right.

Elevators
When the elevators are lowered the air stream is pushed down, the tail rises, and the plane dives.

Flaps
Lowering the flaps increases the curve of the wing giving more lift at take off. They are also used when landing to cause drag as the aircraft is slowing down.

Passenger carriers

The powerful jet engine has made it possible for aircraft to carry large numbers of passengers and cargo all around the world in safety and comfort.

Concorde

Designed and built by Britain and France together, Concorde is the world's fastest passenger aircraft. Flying at 2,170 kph (1,348 mph), Concorde can fly from Paris to New York in 3 ½ hours with up to 139 passengers. Concorde's nose can be raised or lowered, depending on the stage of flight.

Landing and take off

Cruising

Slower speeds

Boeing 747

Known as the 'Jumbo', this huge aircraft can carry more passengers than any other, over 500.

It has two decks and its four engines give it a top speed of 969 kph (602 mph).

Lear Jet

This sleek little two-engined jet can only carry ten passengers. It is mainly used by large companies for business travel.

Military aircraft

The search for bigger, faster jet fighters has produced some amazing aircraft.

Lockheed SR-71A

In 1976 the SR-71A reached a speed of 3,529 kph (2,193 mph) making it the fastest aircraft in the world.

US AIR FORCE

F14 Tomcat

This large, heavy jet fighter takes off and returns to an aircraft carrier.

The Harrier

This is a vertical take off and landing (VTOL) aircraft. It can thrust its jet engines downwards and then backwards.

Helicopters

The helicopter is a wonderful machine. It does not have the speed of a normal plane, but it can go anywhere and do work that no other aircraft can.

The helicopter does not have wings, it has a large rotor on top that is like a propeller, each blade of the rotor can be tilted to give lift.

The whole spinning rotor can then be tilted and the helicopter will move off in that direction, forwards, sideways, even backwards. The little rotor on the tail stops the aircraft from spinning like a top.

With the rotor blades spinning flat there is no lift

When the blade is tilted the helicopter rises up

Communication

Early humans had no written language so we are not really sure how they talked to each other. They may have used signs, or imitated noises made by animals and birds. These simple sounds may have been the beginnings of language.

Written Records

From the earliest times, people needed to keep records. About 5,000 years ago, when ancient people wanted to write something down, they drew a simple picture.

North American Indians used signs. These mean 'friend' and 'horse'.

Cuneiform Writing

Sumerians made wedge-shaped marks in a tablet of soft-clay. This was later baked in the Sun.

Hieroglyphics

Priests in ancient Egypt drew simple pictures to represent words. They wrote on papyrus, a paper made from flattened reeds that grew on the banks of the Nile.

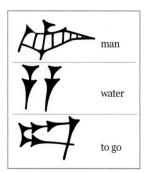
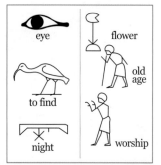

Alphabets

Later on, letters and symbols instead of pictures were used for each different sound in a word. All these different letters made up an alphabet. Here are some different ones:

АБВГДЕЖ
Russian letters

ABΓΔEZHΘIKΛMNΞ
Greek letters

אבגדהוזחטיכלם
Hebrew letters

Sending Messages

Before the invention of the telephone, people had many ways of sending messages: smoke signals, beacon fires, beating drums. Here are some others:

Morse Code – a system of dots and dashes for letters. These could be tapped out, or flashed as long or short light signals.

Semaphore The flag positions represent different letters of the alphabet. This method, used by the army and navy, didn't work in fog or darkness.

Hand spelling – used by deaf people to make words.

Braille – letters made of raised dots that can be felt by blind people.

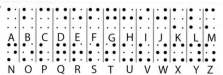

Make your own code. Here is a simple code that you can use with friends. Agree with them on a 'keyword' such as 'father' (or any other word). Now write it out, followed by the rest of the alphabet, in order, but without the keyword letters.

F A T H E R B C D G I J K L M N O P Q S U V W X Y Z
A B C D E F G H I J K L M N O P Q R S T U V W X Y Z

Write the full alphabet beneath. To make your words use the top letters instead of the real ones, so 'Hello Paul' would read 'CEJJM NFUJ'.

Printing

As early as the 7th century, the Chinese carved word pictures onto blocks of wood. They spread ink on the raised parts, pressed paper on top, peeled it off and made a print.

Later they cut all their words on separate small blocks so they could move them round to make different sentences. This is called moveable type.

Wood letter

Until the 15th century most books were hand written, then copied by monks or scribes. They were very rare and expensive, but in those days very few people could read or write.

Then in 1450, Johannes Gutenberg set up the first printing press in Germany. It was made from an old wine press, and it used moveable metal type. The first book that he printed was the Bible. Now books could be made quickly, and this spread new ideas and learning.

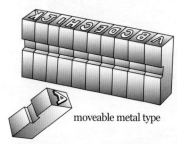

moveable metal type

Gutenberg's method of printing was called 'letterpress'. He could print 300 sheets a day by hand. Modern printers use a system called 'offset lithography'. Huge machines much bigger than a house can print millions of colour pages a day.

Telephones

When Alexander Graham Bell invented a very simple telephone in 1876 he could not have imagined its importance. Today, millions of phone calls are made every day around the world.

When you speak into a phone the sound of your voice is changed into an electrical signal. This signal travels down a wire and is changed back into a voice sound by the phone at the other end. Long distance calls to other countries travel through undersea cables or are bounced off satellites.

Cordless phone
This phone is like the normal one except the two parts are not joined by a cord. The 'base' unit is plugged into a wall socket and receives the call, which it sends on to the handset up to 100 metres away.

Portable phone
These are radio phones that can be taken almost anywhere. Your phone call travels by radio waves to a nearby transmitter, then through the phone wires to a central computer that passes it on to the person you are calling.

Answering Machines

This is like a tape recorder fitted to your telephone. If you are out, it will answer the phone with a taped message that you have made. It will then record the caller's message for you to play back.

Telex

Invented in 1916, this office machine sends typed messages through the telephone lines as electrical signals. They are received by a similar machine that types them out again by itself.

Fax (Facsimile Machines)

Fax machines can send copies of printed material around the world in seconds. They work by transmitting the material through a telephone line. The sender's fax machine scans a document or picture, turns it into electrical signals and sends it like a phone call to another machine anywhere in the world. The receiving fax machine is able to interpret these signals and turn them back into a picture.

—The Computer

The computer is changing our lives faster than anything has ever done before. This machine collects information, sorts it, and stores it in the computer's memory. When you ask it questions, it instantly sorts through the memory and organises all the information in the best way to answer your question in less than a second.

We have been feeding information on every subject into computers for years now. As they can now be linked up to 'talk' to each other, all this information is available in seconds for science, business and education and general use.

disc drive

floppy

Smaller computers store information permanently on floppy disks or CDs.

41

Television

The first regular TV programmes began in London in 1932. These were all in black and white. Colour TV began in America 20 years later.

Television pictures are made by special cameras that change what they see into electrical signals. These are sent to a transmitter that sends them out to be picked up by TV aerials. They then go into our TV set, which turns them back into pictures, all at the speed of light.

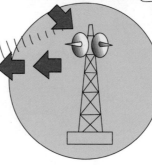

Satellite TV

The first communication satellite was launched in 1952, meaning events happening on one side of the world could be broadcast simultaneously on the other side.

Satellite communication works by bouncing signals off a satellite and back to a point over the Earth's surface. Today there are many satellites in orbit.

Video Cameras

Video cameras (called 'camcorders') record what they see and hear on a small video tape inside the camera. This can be played back immediately through your TV set, or copied on to a normal video tape.

These cameras are often used by companies to make their own films, or by families sending tapes to distant relatives – in fact, anything that is helped by moving pictures.

The Mail Service

When you post a letter it is collected and taken to a sorting office. All the letters are sorted into areas and sent by train to the main town in that area. They are collected in big bags and taken to the post office where they are sorted into streets and roads, then delivered by postmen and women.

Books and Newspapers

Every day, millions of books and newspapers are printed in many languages. Newspapers tell us what is happening in the world and books record information on different subjects. Libraries lend books to the public. They are divided into fiction and non-fiction books and then classified by subject.

Radio

The programmes we hear on the radio are carried to us by radio waves. Just like the TV, sounds are changed into signals, and then back into sounds again when they are picked up by our radio aerial.

The journey into space

About 200km (125 miles) above the Earth's surface the atmosphere fades away to nothing and space begins. There is no air or gravity in space, just a huge emptiness that reaches out to the stars.

The first man-made object to go into space was 'Sputnik 1' launched by the Russians in 1957. In 1961 they launched the first man into space, Colonel Yuri Gagarin.

For the next few years both Russia and America sent men into space. In 1969, the greatest event happened. America landed two men on the moon, Neil Armstrong and Buzz Aldrin, and brought them safely back to Earth.

Here are some of the early spacecraft.

Sputnik 1
Weighed only 85kg (187lbs) - 1957

Gemini
The first two-man craft

Apollo
The first spacecraft to orbit the Moon

Vostok
Russia's first manned spacecraft 1961

Mercury
The first US manned craft

Soyuz
Russian spacecraft

The three stage rocket
The space rocket is like three rockets one on top of another. All of the fuel in stage one is burned up in minutes so the great weight of the engines and fuel tank can fall away into the sea below. Stages two and three continue the journey to orbit height.

The Rocket
To put any craft into space takes enormous power. The American Saturn V rocket has the power of 50 747 Jumbo Jets and travels at 40,000 kph (25,000 mph) to break out of the Earth's gravity.

The space suit
The people who travel in space are called 'astronauts' or 'cosmonauts'.

They must wear special suits when they leave the capsule. The suit has an air supply for breathing – it also protects them from the freezing cold or the direct heat of the Sun.

Mission badges
These embroidered badges are designed for every new space mission that America launches. The astronauts wear them on their space suits.

Capsule

Third stage

Second stage

First stage

Liquid oxygen tank

Kerosene tank

Engines

Capsule

Stage 3

Stage 2

Stage 1

APOLLO

SPACE SHUTTLE

Burning fuel in the rocket engines creates gases. The gases escaping down and out of the engines create an equal force upwards. This is what lifts the great weight of the rocket.

43

The space shuttle

The American space shuttle is the world's first reusable spacecraft. It is launched on the back of a huge fuel tank with a rocket on each side.

When the rockets have done their job they drift back to Earth. The giant fuel tank, which cannot be reused, is allowed to crash.

The shuttle orbits in space to do its work. Most of its body is made up of a big cargo hold with large doors that open for delivery, repairing or recovering satellites. The astronauts go out of these doors to work in space.

When the work is done the shuttle uses its engines to re-enter Earth's atmosphere and then glides back to Earth like a normal aircraft.

From launch to landing

When the rockets and fuel tank fall away the shuttle floats, as there is no gravity in space. The engines slow down the craft to enter Earth's atmosphere. The shuttle pilot then has to glide without power down to land.

Transporting the shuttle

The shuttle is mounted on the fuel tank along with the rockets inside the 'vehicle assembly building' – one of the largest buildings in the world.

It is then carried to the launch pad on the world's biggest and slowest vehicle, the crawler. It weighs 3,000 tonnes and travels at 1.6kph (1mph) but, amazingly, the driver still has to wear a seat belt.

Satellites

A satellite is any object that orbits (goes around) a larger object. The Moon is a natural satellite of the Earth. A large number of man-made satellites now circle the Earth giving us information about the weather, problems on Earth, and help with communications around the world through TV, telephone etc. They also help ships and aircraft to navigate.

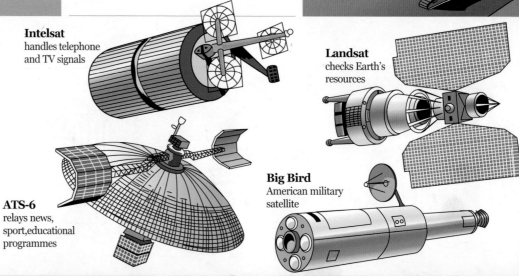

Intelsat
handles telephone and TV signals

Landsat
checks Earth's resources

ATS-6
relays news, sport, educational programmes

Big Bird
American military satellite